Lunch for Patch

by Aysha Davies • illustrated by Christine Battuz

Once upon a time, a rabbit helped his pal, Patch. Patch had six eggs in a nest.

"Patch will like a jam sandwich!"
said Chad. "Patch will want chips!"

Chad put the sandwich and chips in a basket.

"Patch will love this lunch!"

When Chad got to the nest he yelled, "Patch! Here is lunch!"

PATCH

"Is that a bug lunch?" Patch asked. "Little chicks love bugs."

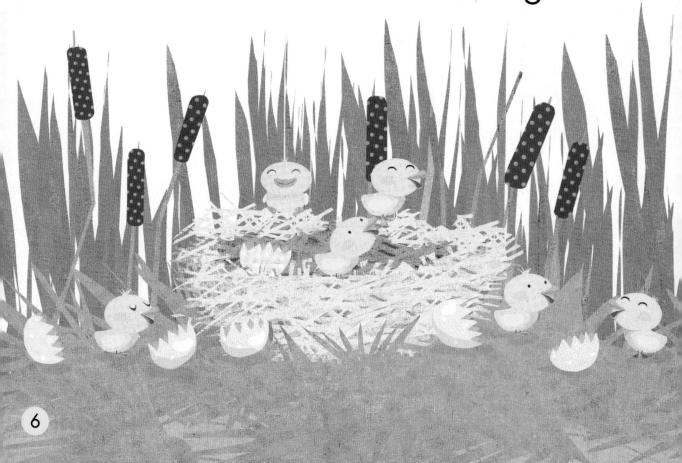

Six chicks said, "Bugs, yes!
Yum!" Chad got bugs.

Patch had the jam sandwich and chips. Six chicks had bugs.